Me and my family

Devised by Jean Maye

British Association for Adoption & Fostering
(BAAF)
Saffron House
6–10 Kirby Street
London EC1N 8TS
www.baaf.org.uk

Charity registration 275689 (England and Wales)
and SC039337 (Scotland)

British Library Cataloguing in Publication Data
A catalogue record for this book is available from the British Library

ISBN 978 1 907585 37 1

Project management by Shaila Shah, Director of Publications, BAAF
Photograph on cover from www.iStockphoto.com
Designed and typeset by Helen Joubert Design
Printed in Great Britain by The Lavenham Press

BAAF is the leading UK-wide membership organisation for all those
concerned with adoption, fostering and child care issues.

Acknowledgements

Me and My Family is dedicated to a friend, Lucy, and her mother. Erica adopted Lucy and her older brother when they were very young. Since the age of eleven, I have been inspired by their family. I have admired the love, warmth and wonderful approach that Erica and her late husband had towards their own and visiting children, including me. If not for them, I doubt that I would have ever thought about pursuing a career in social work with a particular interest in family finding.

I am grateful to the many children and families I have known who have been directly affected by fostering and adoption. Working with them has cemented my learning and understanding of the complexities and dynamics of transitions for children moving to new families.

My sincere thanks and appreciation go again to Shaila Shah at BAAF for her continued confidence in my writing and ideas, and her ability to tune in to my projects, make an input, and work collaboratively with me. Thank you for creating a wonderful book. Thanks also to Jo Francis for her help, to all the readers who commented on earlier drafts, and to Lynda Durrant at Helen Joubert Design for the wonderful design.

Finally, I give my sincerest thanks to Hedi Argent for acting as my editor, fixing all of my grammatical errors and sharing her own expertise. It has been an absolute pleasure working with her.

Note about the author

Jean Maye is a qualified social worker and has been working with children since 1986. She has held various management positions prior to working as a freelance social work consultant and writer. She is also an experienced respite carer for disabled children.

Previous books published by the author under her previous name of Jean Camis are: *My Life and Me* and *We are Fostering*, both published by BAAF, and *When I'm Away From Home,* published by Jessica Kingsley Publications.

During the course of the author's work and research she has continued to identify gaps in available tools when working directly with children and their families. Her workbooks have been written in the attempt to bridge these gaps and to help children make sense of their lives and the changes and challenges that they sometimes face.

Contents

This is me

This book belongs to ....

Introduction

Me and My Family is a book to help you and your new family to get to know each other and for you to record some of the changes in your life when you move and settle with your new family.

The book is divided into three parts. In the first part, your new family can tell you a bit about themselves and stick in photos so that you will be able to recognise them when you meet them and get to know them better. They can also describe their home, where they live and what they do. The second part is for you and your new family to keep a kind of diary about your move, adapting to the changes around you, and settling in. The third part is for you to fill in when something special happens, or you meet your new neighbours, or make new friends, or want to mark birthdays, and anything else that seems important.

Throughout the book, you can write things, stick in photos and draw pictures. And of course, so can members of your family.

This is your book. Enjoy using it and have fun along the way.

INTRODUCING OURSELVES AND
WELCOMING YOU

This is a photograph we have of you

And this is a photograph of us

We would like you to have this book because we want you to know about the people in your new family before you come to live with us.

Inside this book you will find some pages have already been filled in. We've done this to help you to learn our names and know a little bit about us. But there will be plenty more that you will need to know, so we've left blank spaces for any questions you want to ask. We will be very happy to tell you more about ourselves, our lives and our family history.

Name
....

Name
....

Name
....

Name
....

4

The people in the photograph are

....
....
....
....
....

You'll be coming to live with us soon. You must be wondering what your new home is like!

Your new home has .... bedrooms and ....

....
....
....
....
....

This is a photograph of your room. Once you move in with us, you might like to change the colour of your room or move things around. We will help you do that.

Perhaps you could start having a think about what you would like in your bedroom. You could make a list and write it down here.

In my bedroom, I'd like to have:

Our local area

Once you are settled, we can explore the local area together: our shops, our park, the leisure centre and other places.

What sort of places do you go to in your local area?

_____

_____

_____

_____

_____

Where do you like going to best?

_____

_____

_____

_____

_____

When you're living with us, these are some of the local places we can go to together:

_____

_____

_____

_____

_____

What else would you like to know about the area where you are going to live?

Can you think of some questions that you would like to ask us when we meet?

Answers to your questions

_____
_____
_____
_____
_____
_____
_____
_____
_____

Messages to you!

Welcoming you into our family is going to be the most wonderful thing for all of us. Here are our welcoming messages to you:

People in our family

Here are some more photographs of other people in the family.

My name is
....

and
....

....

....

Date
....

My name is
....
and
....

....

....

Date
....

My name is

and

Date

My name is ....

and ....

....

....

....

Date ....

The pets in our family

☐ We don't have any pets.

☐ We have some pets. This is who they are and what they're like!

Our pets

Now we have told you about our family, it's over to you!
You can fill in the next pages yourself or we can fill them in together.

Going to school

When you are ready to go to school, or nursery or playgroup, we will choose one that is right for you. And we will help you to get used to it. Going to a new place can feel a bit scary. But it can also be exciting! What do you think and feel about this?

....

....

....

....

....

....

....

....

Keeping healthy

Keeping well and staying healthy is important so we will look after you and take you to our doctor, dentist or optician, whenever you need to see them.

Our doctor's name is:

Our dentist's name is:

Our local optician is:

Other medical person / people whom you may see:

Meeting my new family

This is a photograph of me with my new family

This photograph was taken by .... on ....

We like this photograph because ....

....

The people in this photograph are:

....

....

....

Meeting a new family can be a bit scary! It can be difficult to remember who you met and where, and what everyone's names are. The diary on the next page can help.

My introductions diary

week	date	who I met	where we met	what we did
1				
2				
3				
4				

Other things I would like to say about our introductions

week 1

week 2

week 3

week 4

other

What did the introductions feel like?

Draw a picture, make a map or write something about your introductions to your new family. Perhaps you could ask someone from your new family to help you.

Date
....

Preparing to move

Moving from one place to another can be tough. If you've stayed in one place for a long time, it can be sad to leave. You'll probably miss familiar things, your routines, and the people around you. But remember, when you belong to a new family, it's for keeps. We'll always be there for you.

So it's understandable if you're feeling nervous about moving. And you must have lots of questions.

Your things

Moving doesn't mean having to leave your things behind! Write down what you'd like to bring with you.

Things I would like to bring

Saying goodbye

Use this page to write down how you said goodbye to people who are important to you and how they said goodbye to you.

Date
....

...is never easy

Use these pages to stick in any letters, cards or messages you have from the people you are saying goodbye to. Or you could keep them all in a special box. Perhaps you could ask someone from your new family to help you.

keeping in touch

Moving to your new family doesn't mean that you will lose touch with old friends and family. Here is a page for you to put all the names and details of the people you want to stay in touch with.

name

address

telephone

email

name

address

telephone

email

name

address

telephone

email

name

address

telephone

email

name

address

telephone

email

name

address

telephone

email

name

address

telephone

email

name

address

telephone

email

Celebrating
your move to a new home and family!

What will you do?

Who will be there?

MOVING IN...
GETTING TO KNOW EACH OTHER

Getting to know each other

There will be new things to get used to – new routines and new family rules. But no one will expect you to learn everything straight away. We will get to know you and you will get to know us over time. How do you spend your weekdays and what do you do at weekends?

	What you do	Is it fun?	Would you like to do that here?
On weekdays			
At weekends			

Settling in to your new home with your new family will take time

This is a picture of me and my new family in our home
....

What we did on this day
....
....
....
....

Date
....

Settling in

Making time for each other and talking about your day or the way you feel will help your new family to understand how you are and what is important to you.

The rest of this book is for you to complete with the help of your new family. Filling it in may take time. It does not have to be done all at once. There are lots of questions in the book that you can ask and lots of things you can tell your new family about yourself.

My moving day

The week day of my move was on a

The month I moved in was

And the year was

My date of birth is

so I was   years and   months

on the day that I moved to live with my new family.

On the day that I moved the weather was

and I was wearing

Other things I want to say about this day:

Date

My favourite things

To get to know you better, we'd like to know what you like and what you don't like. You can use the space below to tell us and add anything else you might like.

What I like and what I don't like

	What I like	What I don't like
Foods		
Drinks		
Games		
Stories		
TV programmes		
Things to do at home		
Things to do outside		
Rules		
Routines		
Anything else?		

Things I'd like to say or draw about my new home and where we live.

This is another photograph of me and some more people in my new family.

The people in this photograph are
....
....
....

This photograph was taken by
....
on
....

The place was
....
....

This is what me and my family did this day:
....
....
....
....
....
....
....
....

My new family name

My parents' full names are:

_____

_____

Other names or nicknames they are known by are:

_____

These names were chosen because:

_____

_____

My full name now is:

_____

My names were chosen because:

_____

_____

Will your name change when you are adopted? Ask your parents what it will be.

My new name when I am adopted will be:

_____

_____

What I would like to say about this:

_____

_____

_____

_____

Date

_____

Changes

Now you've moved into your new home with your family, you may feel very strange at first. It may feel very different from what you have been used to, particularly in the beginning. In these shapes you can say how you are feeling about being there and settling in.

Getting used to changes

Sometimes change can be exciting but also worrying. Use this page to write down anything that is worrying you and what you think might help you to feel better about it.

Perhaps you could talk about it with your family and ask them to help you?

This is what's worrying me

This is what will make me feel better about it

Getting to know everyone in the family can be confusing, especially if your new family is very big!

On this page you can make a list of as many people in your new family as you can remember!
Ask your parents whether you have left anyone out.

First name	Family name	Relation / who they are	Where they live

What about asking for a new address book so that you can put in it all the names and addresses of your new family and friends?

My family's birthdays and where they were born

Name	Date of birth	Birthplace

Ups and downs

Any family can have its ups and downs when there are changes. Talk to your family and share your thoughts and feelings about your adoption. Use the questions and spaces below to help you.

What has changed in the family?	Thoughts and feelings
My family's thoughts and feelings	What I don't understand

Questions!

Answers

what's best?

what's great?

what's not so great?

what has got better now?

My new school/nursery

The place we have chosen is

....

And this is a photograph / drawing of

I will be starting on

....

and at the time I will be .... years old and .... months.

Something I would like to say about starting my new school / nursery:

....

....

This is what my family and I will do to get ready:

....

....

My adoptive parents

Ask your parents to tell you about their lives and background. Ask them if they have any photographs of their childhoods, school days, growing up, or family celebrations to stick in the spaces below. Write in your own headings or ask your parents to write them.

What I have found out about my adoptive parents

Where they have worked

What their jobs are

Where they have lived

Where they came from

What else I've learnt about my adoptive parents

....

....

....

Things we have learnt about each other

You can use these spaces to write down some of the things that you and your family have learnt about each other. Here's some examples: who likes to go to bed early? Who likes to stay up late? Who doesn't like washing up? Who does most of the housework? Who prepares the meals? Who makes the most noise? Who keeps their room tidy?

My new family's hobbies and interests

In the spaces below, write in your family's favourite hobbies and interests, i.e. what they like to do – swimming, football, playing computer games, gardening, etc. And then, write your own...

My own hobbies and interests

Other family members

Who else is in your new family? Grandparents? Aunties and uncles? Cousins? Use the space below to stick in photographs of your new relatives. If you have any brothers and sisters, ask them to choose a photograph to give you.

Remember to write everyone's names and who they are!

The people in these photographs are ....

....

....

....

Date ....

My family

In the space below, draw a picture of your new family. Start with the eldest on one side to the youngest on the other. If your family is too big to fit into the frame, try just drawing their faces with their ages underneath.

New grandparents

Grandparents are often very important in a family. Have you got new grandparents?
What are they like? If you do, how about using this page to draw or stick in photographs
and write something about them?

Date

New aunties and uncles

If your parents have any sisters and brothers, they will be your aunties and uncles. Even if your parents don't have any sisters or brothers, other relatives or friends might be like an auntie or an uncle.

Use the space below to stick in photographs of any new aunties or uncles you have and write down something about them below the photographs.

The people in these photographs are

....

....

....

Date ....

The people in these photographs are
....
....
....
....
Date
....

New cousins

Cousins are the children of your aunties and uncles. Some children have lots of cousins and some have none. If you have new cousins, you can fill in their names here.

Name of cousin	Their parents' names	Something about them

Our family tree

A common way of finding out and remembering who's who in the family is to draw a family tree. Ask your family to help you to do this in the space below. Remember that a tree can have many branches.

What about getting a large piece of paper or card and making a family collage of photographs to hang on the wall? Don't forget to include yourself!

New friends

Sometimes you can make friends quickly. Sometimes making new friends can take a little time. When you make new friends, perhaps you would like to use this page to write their names and to say something about them.

Do they have a nickname?
How old are they?
Do they live near you?
Do they have any sisters or brothers?
Do they have a pet?

My new friends

Perhaps they will give you a photograph to stick in or you can draw them?

Neighbours

Moving home also means meeting new people outside of the family, including neighbours. Sometimes neighbours can also be friends and sometimes not. We should always be polite and pleasant to the people who live close to us, even if they are not our friends. Have you met the neighbours yet? When you meet them, you can use the space below to write their names and anything interesting about them. Or you can draw them and where they live.

My thoughts and feelings

Use the next two pages to write or draw your happy thoughts and your sad thoughts. Perhaps you would like to talk to your new family and do something together?

My happy thoughts and feelings

My sad thoughts and feelings

Things I'd like to do with my new family

What kinds of things would you like to do with your new family, to help you get to know each other a bit better? You can make a list below.

Date

My Adoption Day

The next section is all about living together as a family and planning for your future, but before you go on, it is important to say something about your actual adoption day. This will help you to understand what made this day special and to remember this day in the future. What was the date? Where did you celebrate? What was everyone wearing? If you have pictures, you can stick them in below!

This is a photograph of the law courts where I was adopted.

Who was there?

....

....

....

....

....

The law court was in   The date of the hearing was

....

Names of the people present   Who they are   What they said

....

....

....

....

....

Use this page to write or draw anything else you would like to say about your adoption day.

Date

This is how we celebrated
my adoption

HAPPY ADOPTION DAY!

This is a copy of my adoption certificate.

LIVING TOGETHER

Part of the family

Now you are adopted you are part of our family forever. Living together means looking out for each other and respecting each other. Sharing and caring are also important. Sometimes family life is easy and sometimes it isn't quite so easy, especially when you are still getting to know one another. Perhaps this book has already helped you to know each other a little better, but you can go on learning about your family all your life!

This final part of the book is for you to complete as and when you feel like it, so don't try to do it all at once! It is for you to keep a record of your life in the family: the things you do together, the special occasions, holidays, special achievements, the days you want to remember.

What becoming a family has meant to us

Talk to your family and ask everyone to write in one of the spaces what being part of the family means to them. Don't forget to do it yourself.

Things I have found out about my family by living together

What we know about each other's likes and dislikes

How we help each other

Talk to members of your family about how you have helped each other out recently. This might have been with filling in this workbook, or helping with homework, or you might have looked after someone when they weren't well, or someone may have comforted you when you were a bit sad.

What I have done to help someone in the family

What someone in the family has done to help me

64

Things that bring us closer together

Things we enjoy doing together as a family

Date
....

Going to school

What I like about going to school is

....
....
....
....

What I don't like about going to school is

....
....
....

My teachers are

....
....
....

Classmates I like

....
....
....
....
....

New friends I have made

....
....
....

These are the after school activities I do

....
....
....

Date
....

66

What are some of the new things you are learning?
You can write about them or draw pictures below.

A week in our life

Every day is different but some days can be more like other days. For example, every week there's some school days and every week has a weekend. What happens in a normal week in your family? Pick a week and write down what happened and what you did.

Day	date	what we did
Mon		
Tues		
Weds		
Thurs		
Fri		
Sat		
Sun		

New hobbies and activities

Use this page to write, draw or stick in photographs of any of the hobbies and activities you take part in or are learning to do, or want to learn about.

A family day to remember

All families have special days that they remember. It could be a birthday, a family outing or another special occasion. Can you remember one?

Remembering and sharing the sad times

It's important to remember good times as well as bad. What makes you sad? What made you sad before you moved to your new family?

I'd feel less sad if...

Perhaps you could share this with your parents. Together, you could write down what would make you less sad.

Happy things that have happened recently

It's lovely to hear nice things about yourself! And it's lovely to say nice things about others. On this page, you and others in your family can write nice things you'd like to say to each other.

A happy poem or song we like in this family

74

Family celebrations!

Birthdays, anniversaries, your Adoption Day, holidays and other special days...
you can make a calendar of family celebrations.

January

February

March

April

May

June

July

August

September

October

November

December

Special events

In the spaces below, make a note of some of the special events or special days you are looking forward to.

Name of event
....

When
....

Where
....

What will you do on that day?
....
....
....
....
....

Name of event
....

When
....

Where
....

What will you do on that day?
....
....
....
....
....

Name of event
....

When
....

Where
....

What will you do on that day?
....
....
....
....

Name of event
....

When
....

Where
....

What will you do on that day?
....
....
....
....

Make a wishlist!

We all have hopes and dreams and wishes for the future. What are yours?

My wishlist

Get your family to make their wishlist!

Everyone has wishlists! Get people in your family to write theirs too!

Remembering family events

YEAR	Special things I would like to remember

YEAR   Special things I would like to remember

These last pages are for you to add whatever
you want, whenever you feel like it.

This book is for you to keep and will help you to remember everything you want to remember about the time you met your new family and were adopted.

If you need more space you can always start another book!

Other BAAF books that you may like to read

There are lots of books that you can read about adoption when you are young, but also when you are grown up. Below is a very short list of some of them, but you can ask your parents to help you look for others on our website at **www.baaf.org.uk**, or on **www.amazon.co.uk**.

Adoption: What it is and what it means, **by Shaila Shah**
A guide for young children which explains what adoption means, with definitions of puzzling new words

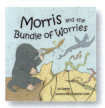

Morris and the Bundle of Worries, **by Jill Seeney**
A colourful picture book which looks at how Morris the mole learns to deal with his big bundle of worries.

Elfa and the Box of Memories, **by Michelle Bell**
A colourful picture book which follows Elfa the elephant as she sets out to recapture some of her lost memories.

The Most Precious Present in the World, **by Becky Edwards**
Mia, who is adopted, wants to know why she looks different to her adoptive parents. This picture book explains how it is OK to have mixed feelings about adoption.

The Nutmeg series, **by Judith Foxon**
This series of six books follows Nutmeg the squirrel and his brother and sister as they have to leave their birth parents, and are adopted by another squirrel family. Each book looks at a different aspect of adoption, including difficult feelings, life story work and school issues.

Josh and Jaz have Three Mums, **by Hedi Argent**
This brightly illustrated book tells the story of Josh and Jaz, young twins who are adopted by a lesbian couple.

Dad David, Baba Chris and Me, **by Ed Merchant**
A colourful picture book about Ben, who is teased at school for having two dads, and how his teacher helps him and his class to understand that children live in all sorts of families.

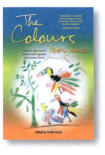

The Colours in Me, **edited by Perlita Harris**
A collection of personal stories, writings and artwork from adopted children and young people, including some work from intercountry adopted children.

A support network you might like to know about

Talk Adoption: www.talkadoption.org.uk

We are here to listen and help.

You know what it's like...don't want to talk to your parents and can't really talk to your friends. Maybe it doesn't feel right to talk to a teacher or anyone else. Call us instead. We are here to listen about what adoption means to you. So if you live in the UK and have a connection of any kind to adoption, call us.

Talk Adoption is the UK's only freephone national helpline for young people with a connection to adoption.

You can contact us on 0808 808 1234 or actiononline@afteradoption.org.uk.

Life after adoption

Year	Things I'd like to say or remember
January	
February	
March	
April	
May	
June	
July	
August	
September	
October	
November	
December	

Life after adoption

Year	Things I'd like to say or remember
January	
February	
March	
April	
May	
June	
July	
August	
September	
October	
November	
December	

Life after adoption

Year	Things I'd like to say or remember
January	
February	
March	
April	
May	
June	
July	
August	
September	
October	
November	
December	

Life after adoption

If you need more space you can always start another book or journal.

Year	Things I'd like to say or remember
January	
February	
March	
April	
May	
June	
July	
August	
September	
October	
November	
December	